SCHOLASTIC

25 Easy NONFICTION MINI-BOOKS

by Judy Nayer

NEW YORK • TORONTO • LONDON • AUCKLAND • SYDNEY
MEXICO CITY • NEW DELHI • HONG KONG • BUENOS AIRES

Teaching Resources

For Matthew

Scholastic Inc. grants teachers permission to photocopy the mini-books in this collection for classroom use. No other part of this publication may be reproduced in whole or in part, or stored in a retrieval system, or transmitted in any form or by any means, electronic, mechanical, photocopying, recording, or otherwise, without written permission of the publisher. For information regarding permissions, write to Scholastic Inc., 557 Broadway, New York, NY 10012-3999.

Cover design by Maria Lilja

Cover and interior illustrations by Anne Kennedy

Interior design by Sydney Wright

ISBN: 0-439-46603-2
Copyright © 2005 by Judy Nayer
All rights reserved. Published by Scholastic Inc.
Printed in the U.S.A.

5 6 7 8 9 10   40   14 13 12 11 10 09 08

Contents

Science Mini-Books

Social Studies Mini-Books

Math Mini-Books

Introduction

Reading nonfiction books is a great way for children to expand their knowledge, build vocabulary, and satisfy their natural curiosity about the world around them. But most informational books are far too complex for beginning readers. That's why I've written these nonfiction mini-books that even the youngest readers can read themselves. In *25 Easy Nonfiction Mini-Books*, children can gain confidence practicing their reading skills as they learn about essential topics in three content areas: science, social studies, and math. These reproducible, easy-to-read books have all the features that support emergent readers: simple text, rhyme, repetition, and illustrations that closely match the text. The topics have been correlated to the standards (see page 5), so you can easily integrate content into your reading instruction—a teaching approach that is both fun and practical!

Here are some ways you can use these mini-books in your classroom:

* to provide content reading on a theme your class is studying

* to introduce a topic or thematic unit

* to encourage children to read independently in school and at home

* to inspire children's own writing

* to launch a research project

* to encourage children to select books about topics that are of interest to them

* to allow children to create their own mini-book libraries

To reinforce the science, social studies, and math concepts in each mini-book, on pages 6–14 I have included ideas for classroom activities to launch or follow up the readings. These include discussion suggestions, hands-on projects, and writing ideas to engage children and enrich their learning. In addition, each of these pages includes a list of related trade books for read-aloud and independent reading.

I hope that the children in your class will enjoy these nonfiction mini-books especially written for them. I also hope that as children learn to read, these books will awaken them to the experience of *reading to learn*.

Happy reading! And happy learning!

—*Judy Nayer*

How to Make the Mini-Books

1. Remove the mini-book pages from the book along the vertical perforated lines. Make a double-sided copy of each page on 8$\frac{1}{2}$- by 11-inch paper.

2. Cut each page in half along the solid line. You should have 8 pages (including the cover) for each mini-book.

3. Place page 2 behind the title page.

4. Fold the pages in half along the dotted line. Check to be sure that the pages are in the proper order, and then staple them together along the book's spine. Invite children to color the books, as desired.

NOTE: If you do not wish to make double-sided copies, you can photocopy single-sided copies of each page, cut apart the mini-book pages, and stack them together in order, with the title page on top. Then staple the pages together along the left-hand side.

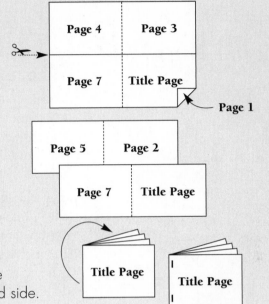

How to Use the Mini-Books

The nonfiction mini-books in this collection can be used in any order for shared reading, guided reading, paired or independent reading, and take-home reading. You may wish to begin each book as a shared reading experience, modeling the reading process and discussing new vocabulary and concepts as you read the mini-book aloud to the whole class. For repeated readings, have children work in small groups, with a partner or older student buddy, or individually. Invite children to color the illustrations in each mini-book and to store their mini-books in decorated shoe boxes or folders. You may also wish to provide copies of the mini-books in theme-based learning centers around the classroom. Encourage children to write their own nonfiction books to add to their mini-book libraries.

Connections to the Language Arts Standards

The activities in this book are designed to support you in meeting the following K–2 reading standards outlined by Mid-continent Research for Education and Learning (McRel), an organization that collects and synthesizes national and state K–12 curriculum standards.

Use the general skills and strategies of the reading process:
- Uses mental images and meaning clues based on pictures and print to aid in comprehension of text
- Uses basic elements of phonetic and structural analysis to decode unknown words
- Understands level-appropriate sight words and vocabulary
- Uses self-correction strategies
- Uses reading skills and strategies to understand a variety of informational texts
- Understands the main idea and supporting details of simple expository information
- Summarizes information found in texts (retells in own words)
- Relates new information to prior knowledge and experience

Source—*Content Knowledge: A Compendium of Standards and Benchmarks for K–12 Education* (4th ed.). (Mid-continent Research for Education and Learning, 2004)

Classroom Activities

Science

Where Do Animals Live?

Explain to children that animals can live in many different kinds of places. Ask them to brainstorm a list of animals, and write their ideas on the board. Then ask children to name the place where each animal lives. As you read the mini-book with children, review each place that is mentioned and the animals that live there.

After reading, divide the class into groups. Privately assign each group one of the following habitats: woods, pond, rain forest, farm, desert, sea, a person's home. Ask children to keep these places a secret from the other groups. Then invite children to work in their groups to prepare a role-play that shows the animals in their homes. How do the animals sound? How do they look and move? Invite each group to share its role-play, as the rest of the class tries to guess the habitat.

How a Seed Grows

After reading the mini-book, invite children to plant and observe the growth of their own bean plants.

1. Help children fill clear plastic cups with potting soil. Have them press a bean seed (lima beans and string beans work well) into the center of the soil.

2. Assist children in adding a small amount of water to their cups.

3. Have them write their names on sticky notes and attach them to their cups.

4. Set the cups in an area that gets sun. Have children check the cups daily, adding water when the soil feels dry.

5. Give children an observation sheet that contains four panels: Day 1, Day 5, Day 10, and Day 15. Have children complete the first panel by drawing how their plants look on the first day. Continue this process on the fifth, tenth, and fifteenth days of growth. Can children see any roots? What is happening to the bean seed?

6. On the final day, invite children to share their panels. As a class, write a paragraph about the stages of growth observed.

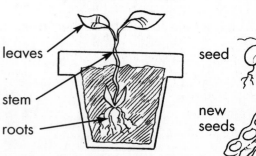

Parts of a Plant

leaves

stem

roots

seed

new seeds

Read More!

A House for Hermit Crab by Eric Carle (Simon & Schuster, 1991). As Hermit Crab searches for a new house, children learn about the habits of hermit crabs and other animals that live in the sea environment.

With bright, bold illustrations, *Growing Vegetable Soup* by Louis Ehlert (Harcourt, 1987) shares the experiences of a gardener who plants and harvests a vegetable garden and then uses the vegetables in a soup.

Everything Changes

Discuss with children the concept that things change. Demonstrate changes by: 1) leaving an ice cube in a glass for half an hour; 2) blowing up a balloon; and 3) blowing bubbles and popping them. Brainstorm a list of other changes children have observed.

✳ Then invite children to create an "Everything Changes" book. Have them fold a sheet of paper in half width-wise. Write the words "Before," "During," and "After" on the chalkboard. Ask children to copy "Before" onto the cover of their books, "During" onto the first page, and "After" onto the last page. Then have them create three illustrations that show the stages of one of the changes you discussed or demonstrated.

✳ Have children bring in pictures of themselves as babies. Create a bulletin board display, and invite children to guess the identities of the babies posted. How have children changed? You may wish to expand the activity by having children create timelines of their lives using photographs of themselves at different ages and stages.

Who Is Hiding?

Remind children that the mini-book *Where Do Animals Live?* showed big places where animals lived, such as ponds, rain forests, deserts, and seas. Explain that there are smaller places within those places—things like caves, nests, and plants—which can be homes for animals, too. As you read the mini-book, have children notice the animal homes, pointing out how the homes protect and hide the animals.

Discuss another way animals hide—through camouflage. Tape a colored sheet of bulletin board paper against a wall. Have a child who is wearing clothing that is not the same color stand against the sheet. Ask children if the child is easy to see. Why? Then have a child wearing the same color as the sheet of paper stand against it. Now what happens? Explain to children that the child is camouflaged. Tell them that camouflage is a special coloring or pattern that some animals have that allows them to blend in with an environment. It helps them hide from enemies and to hide from animals they are hunting. Using this concept, supply children with art materials and invite them to create pictures of animals that are camouflaged by their backgrounds.

Water, Water Everywhere!

Use the pages of the mini-book to discuss the many ways in which we use water—for washing, cooking, cleaning, drinking, and recreation. Ask children to think of other specific uses for water, such as putting out fires, helping plants grow, feeding pets, washing floors and clothes, brushing teeth, filling swimming pools, and so on.

Read More!

Born to Be a Butterfly by Karen Wallace (DK, 2002). Through eye-catching layouts and striking photos, children follow the transformation of a caterpillar as it becomes a Red Admiral butterfly. Also in the series: *Duckling Days* and *Tale of a Tadpole*.

Animals are on the prowl in *Pop-Up: Hide and Seek* (National Geographic, 1999). Movable spreads depict the ways their camouflage enables them to hunt for food.

With beautiful illustrations and poetic text, *Water Dance* by Thomas Locker (Harcourt, 1997) presents a lyrical view of the water cycle.

Read More!

Whatever the Weather by Karen Wallace (DK, 1999). Part of the DK Readers series, this Level 1 title features a controlled vocabulary and striking visuals. The weather changes from day to day, but William longs for rain.

Joanna Cole explains how the five senses work and provides simple activities for children to try in *You Can't Smell a Flower With Your Ear! All About Your 5 Senses* (Putnam/Grosset, 1994).

Be a Friend to Trees by Patricia Lauber (HarperCollins, 1994). Children learn the many ways that people and animals rely on trees in this fact-filled book.

All Kinds of Weather

After reading the mini-book, you may wish to sing its words to the tune of "London Bridge Is Falling Down." Children can use the illustrations to supply the last word of each verse, or supply their own. For example: *Sunny days are fun for me/fun for me, fun for me./Sunny days are fun for me/I like riding.*

Next, discuss the weather in your area. Ask children to share the things they enjoy doing on sunny, rainy, and snowy days. Then brainstorm words that describe weather, such as *muggy*, *foggy*, *hot*, *chilly*, *dry*, and so on. Write each word on a large index card.

Then set up a weekly weather chart on a bulletin board, and arrange the word cards around it. Let children take turns being the class weather person. Have the weather person draw a picture on the chart that describes the daily weather conditions. Go online as a class to obtain the temperature, or use an outdoor thermometer. Have the weather person add the temperature to the chart and a weather-describing word or words to the chart. Then have him or her present the weather report to the class.

My Five Senses

Discuss the five senses. Ask children to identify the body parts that are used for each. Explain that we often use more than one sense at a time. For example, when we eat an ice cream cone, we see its shape and colors. We smell the scent of mint or chocolate. We feel the cold, creamy ice cream in our mouths and taste the sweet flavor. We hear the cone crunch when we bite into it.

Invite children to use all their senses as they prepare and eat popcorn. If possible, use a hot air popper so that children can watch the process. On the chalkboard, create a three-column chart with the headings, "Before," "During," and "After" for recording children's responses throughout the experience. First, show them the popcorn kernels, and invite them to use words that describe what the kernels look and feel like. Then as the popcorn pops, encourage children to use their ears, eyes, and noses to share what their senses are experiencing. When the popcorn is ready, invite children to use their sense of taste to describe it!

Animals Need Trees

After reading the mini-book, review the living things described and the ways in which they use the tree. Then create a large wall mural of an oak tree. Label the parts, including acorns, leaves, branches, trunk, bark, and roots. Invite children to create cutout drawings to place in the tree to show who needs the tree (for example, animal inhabitants, birds in nests, people picking apples).

Social Studies

What We Like

Discuss with children the concept that there are differences and similarities among people and that each person is special or unique. Then ask children to think about the interests they have and the things they like to do.

Invite them to create a class big book called "What We Like." Write the sentence "_____ likes to _____." on the chalkboard, and ask each student to complete the sentence with his or her name and an activity he or she likes to do. Copy each completed sentence onto its own large sheet of paper and have students create accompanying illustrations for their individual pages. Create a cover for the book and bind it for reading and sharing.

Friends

Ask children to explain what a friend is and to discuss the qualities that make others good friends. Invite them to share ideas about what they like to do with their friends. Then work with children to create a friendship quilt.

1. Give each child a fabric quilt square and colored markers.

2. Ask children to create a drawing on the square that shows them having fun with a friend or that represents something they like to do with a friend. If you wish, supply decorations, such as sequins, beads, and yarn, which children can glue onto their squares.

3. Create a title square labeled "Friends Forever!"

4. Work with students to arrange and glue the completed squares onto a large piece of fabric to create the quilt. You may wish to add a decorative border. Display the completed quilt in the classroom.

My Family

Explain to children that there are many kinds of families and family members, such as immediate and extended families, pets, and so on. Tell them that a family portrait is a special photograph that includes different family members. Invite children to create their own family portraits. Hand out sheets of paper and have children make thumbprints for each of their family members. Then have them use the prints to draw the people and pets that make up their families. Help children label each family member. Then have them glue borders around their pictures to serve as picture frames.

Read More!

I Like Me! by Nancy Carlson (Puffin, 1990) sings the praises of self-esteem. From her curly tail to her tiny little feet, this upbeat little piggy knows just what she likes—herself!

Friends at School by Rochelle Bunnett (Star Bright Books, 1996). A diverse group of children participating in a wide variety of activities convey the fun and friendship of school.

Families Are Different by Nina Pelligrini (Holiday House, 1991). In this reassuring story about traditional and nontraditional families, Nico's adopted mother teaches her that families are joined with "a special kind of glue called love."

Read More!

Fathers, Mothers, Sisters, Brothers: A Collection of Family Poems by Mary Ann Hoberman (Little, Brown, 2001) is a collection of thirty warm and wise poems about many different kinds of families.

What Will I Be? by Wendy Cheyette Lewison (Cartwheel Books, 2001) presents witty photos of children dressed as bakers, firefighters, and other workers, and rhyming riddles that offer hints about the jobs represented.

Bear About Town by Stella Blackstone (Barefoot Books, 2001). Rhyming, patterned language, a loveable bear character, and a map are all part of the fun in this book that visits different places in town each day of the week.

What Do Families Do?

Invite children to brainstorm specific activities families do together in the following categories: work, play, shop, eat, travel, and learn. Then divide the class into six groups and assign each group one of the categories; for example, "Families Work Together." Give each group a stack of magazines. Invite children to locate and cut out photos of family members engaged in their assigned activities. For example, the "Families Work Together" group might locate a photo of a parent and child loading a dishwasher. Children can also locate photos of related objects to add to the collage. For example, the "Families Eat Together" group might include a pizza. Have groups glue their photos onto posterboard to create a collage. Add a title to each completed collage.

When I Grow Up

Prepare a set of "Work ABC Cards," using 9- by 12-inch paper of heavy stock. Write one career for each letter of the alphabet on individual cards. For example: astronaut, bus driver, chef, doctor, electrician, firefighter, grocer, hair stylist, illustrator, jet pilot, kindergarten teacher, librarian, mail carrier, nurse, organist, police officer, quarterback, rescue worker, sales clerk, truck driver, umpire, vet, writer, X-ray technician, yoga instructor, zookeeper.

Discuss with children what they might be when they grow up. Explain that there are many kinds of work that people do. Read each card aloud, asking children to identify the letter of the alphabet with which each job begins. Invite them to share what they already know about each job. Help them locate a few facts about those that are unfamiliar. Assign children specific cards to illustrate, asking them to use in their drawings what they know about the job that each person does.

What's in a Community?

Discuss with children the people and places found in communities. Work with them to create a large wall or floor map that shows the location of key places in their community. Then ask them to answer the following riddles:

✳ You can run on my fields or play on my swings. You can sit on my benches and eat picnic things. What am I? (a park)

✳ My big red trucks are waiting inside. When help is needed, they'll go for a ride. What am I? (a fire station)

✳ Mail a letter, buy some stamps, pick up a special package from Gramps! What am I? (a post office)

✳ Buy food to eat or shoes for your feet. Find toys to have fun with or sales clerks to greet. What are we? (stores)

✳ We can be big or small, we can be old or new. People live in us, and pets do, too! What are we? (houses)

Let's Go!

Invite children to share some of the places they have gone and the methods of transportation they have used to get there. As you read the mini-book with children, discuss the labels on the illustrations. Then work with children to sort various methods of transportation in a pictograph.

1. Have children look through magazines and cut out photos of different methods of transportation, such as buses, cars, or ships.

2. Invite each of the children to create a pictograph called "Let's Go!" Have each draw three columns on a sheet of butcher paper. Write the labels, "Air," "Land," and "Water" on the chalkboard, and have students copy them onto their pictographs as column heads. Invite students to glue the magazine photos under the appropriate column heads.

3. When children have completed their pictographs, ask them to count the total number of items they placed in each column. Work with the whole group to tally grand totals.

Long Ago and Today

Ask children to compare and contrast the past and the present by recalling details from the mini-book. Invite them to discuss the ways families, houses, and towns looked long ago and the way they look today.

Discuss the fact that just as things have changed from long ago to today, today's things will change and be different in the future. Invite children to brainstorm ways that schools, houses, cars, clothes, towns, and other things might change, and what they might be like in years to come. Create a "World of Tomorrow" bulletin board. Have each child draw a picture for the bulletin board that shows an item the way it might appear in the future. Have them label the drawing with the sentence, "This is a _____ of the future." Post the drawings and invite children to take turns telling about them.

America the Beautiful

Ask children to recall the physical features, such as mountains, seas, and deserts, mentioned in the mini-book. Label a map of the United States with stick-on dots to show children the locations of these features. Then invite children and their families to ask caregivers, friends, and other family members who live out-of-state or who travel to other areas to send your class a postcard from a place in the United States. Each time your class receives a postcard, read it aloud, discuss the physical features it contains, and add a dot on the map to mark the location from which it came. Display each card around the map.

Read More!

The fun-filled rhymes in *This Is the Way We Go to School* by Edith Baer (Scholastic, 1992) teach how children from very different cultures around the world get to school.

Sarah Morton's Day and *Samuel Eaton's Day* by Kate Waters (Scholastic, 1989, 1993) invite readers to learn what daily life was like for pilgrim children in the 1600s.

America the Beautiful by Katharine Lee Bates, illustrated by Wendall Minor (Putnam, 2003). Background information on the lyrics of "America the Beautiful" accompanies stunning watercolors that showcase both the physical attributes of the United States and pieces of its history.

Math

Read More!

The Shape of Things by Dayle Ann Dodds (Candlewick, 1996). Clever rhymes and bright, paper-cut illustrations show how basic shapes form houses, boats, and many other everyday objects.

Whether in the threads of a spider's web, in a watermelon's stripes, or in the rings of a tree, patterns found in the natural world are featured in *Lots and Lots of Zebra Stripes: Patterns in Nature* by Stephen R. Swinburne (Boyds Mill Press, 1998).

Eating Pairs: Counting Fruits and Vegetables by Twos by Sarah L. Shuette (Pebble Books, 2003). Children will sink their teeth into this delicious and nutritious approach to counting by twos!

Shape Walk

Review with children the various shapes that the children in the mini-book saw on their shape walk and the items that formed those shapes. Ask them what kinds of shapes they might see on their own shape walk. Then take the class on a brief shape walk through the school building and, if possible, outside.

When you return to the classroom, post four sheets of posterboard on a bulletin board. At the top of each sheet, draw and write the name of one of these shapes: circle, square, rectangle, and triangle. (You should have one sheet for each of the four shapes.) Ask children to name the items they saw on their walk. Then record the items on the appropriate sheet of posterboard and tally the items on each list. Which shape did children see the most? the least? Keep the lists posted and invite children to add items as they discover them.

Patterns

Review with children the visual patterns they saw in the mini-book. Then invite them to make a necklace with a pattern of their choice.

1. Supply children with pieces of yarn and items to string, including colored beads and pieces of dry pasta, such as rigatoni and macaroni. (Let children paint the pasta with different primary colors prior to the activity.)

2. Tell children to devise a special pattern, such as two blue beads, one yellow bead, and two pieces of rigatoni, and string their necklaces.

3. Have children wear their completed necklaces and share them with the group. Ask the group to identify the patterns.

Then challenge children to use their hearing to discover patterns. Tell them to first listen as you clap a pattern, for example, clap, clap, clap, pause/clap, clap, clap, pause. Then ask them to repeat the same clapping pattern. Continue with more complicated patterns, including other motions, such as stamping your feet, tapping your knees, snapping your fingers, and so on.

Let's Count!

Review with children that the girl in the mini-book counted even-numbered items. Ask children to skip count to ten, by twos, along with you. Then invite them to make a wheel of even-numbered items. Supply each child with a paper plate that has been divided into five equal sections. Ask children to write the numerals *2, 4, 6, 8,* and *10,* one in each section, on their plates. Next, provide small items, such as pebbles, shells, beans, seeds, and pasta. Have them glue the appropriate number of items in each section of their wheels.

How Many?

Remind children that in the mini-book they first guessed how many items were pictured; then they went back and counted. Invite children to visit four stations, where they will guess how many items are on display. Prior to the activity, place items such as shells, crayons, paper clips, and pennies at each of four stations. Place a label, such as "Station 1," at each location to identify it. On a sheet of paper, make a four-column chart. Label the columns "Station 1," "Station 2," and so on. Then make a copy for each child. After recording their guesses on their charts children will take them from station to station, where they will count the items to determine if their guesses were correct. Afterward have children review their guesses and final counts. Were their guesses accurate? Which station's items were easiest to guess? hardest?

I Spy

Invite children to join you in a game of "I Spy." Tell them that you will provide three clues about an object in the classroom (or outside if windows are available). Hold up a pair of imaginary binoculars and peer through them. Then give children clues such as "I spy something thin," "I spy something long," and "I spy something yellow." Have them guess the item—in this case, a pencil! After you have provided children with several examples, pass the "binoculars" to volunteers. Have them provide clues as the rest of the group guesses what is being described.

Which Is Bigger?

Review with children the concepts of bigger, smaller, shorter, taller, and longer. Ask children to name other words that compare, such as *harder* and *softer*. Then challenge children to make up their own comparison sentences like the ones in the mini-book. Using classroom items, have children compare items by size and other attributes, for example, "The bookcase is taller than the table."

Then invite children to play an identification game. Prior to the activity, place several pairs of items in paper bags, one pair per bag. Pairs might include a large stuffed animal and a small one and a 12-inch ruler and a 6-inch one. Write "larger, smaller," and "shorter, longer," for example, on the outsides of the bags to indicate their contents. Then invite volunteers to select a bag, cover their eyes, and reach inside. Direct children to remove a particular item from the bag by answering your questions, for example, "Which one is bigger? Which one is longer? Which one is softer?"

Read More!

One, Two, Three, Count With Me by Catherine Anholt and Laurent Anholt (Viking, 1994) is a highly-spirited, rhyming concept book that invites children to count items grouped by size, colors, days of the week, and body parts.

Just one of many titles in the popular I Spy series, *I Spy Treasure Hunt: A Book of Picture Riddles* by Jean Marzollo, photographs by Walter Wick, (Cartwheel Books, 1999) is a visual wonder. Children are challenged to locate objects on a hunt for pirate's treasure.

The NBA Book of Big and Little by James Preller (Scholastic, 1998). With clear text and vivid photos, this concept book with a high-interest twist features the stars of the NBA.

Read More!

One Guinea Pig Is Not Enough by Kate Duke (Puffin, 2001). One lone guinea pig is gradually joined by others in this free-wheeling story. Children use the numerals 1 to 10 to add growing numbers of lovable guinea pigs.

Adding Fun

After reading the mini-book, read it again, but this time have children use simple manipulatives to act out each number sentence in the story. Encourage them to use the manipulatives to make up new stories to share with the class. Write their number sentences on the chalkboard.

Next, invite children to work with partners to play an addition game. Give each pair of children a set of number cubes. Ask them to take turns rolling the cubes. Then ask them to write a number sentence that shows the numbers on the cubes and their added total. For example, if children roll cubes with two dots and six dots, their number sentence will be $2 + 6 = 8$. Encourage children to draw the appropriate number of dots under each number in their number sentences.

It's Time

Prior to reading this mini-book, invite children to create their own personalized clock "faces" to track the time as they read.

1. Give each child a paper plate, markers or crayons, simple hour and minute hands cut from heavy paper, and a brass fastener. Also have yarn and glue available.

2. Guide children in writing the numbers 1–12 around the edge of the paper plate. (Or use a pencil to lightly trace the numbers ahead of time.)

3. Invite them to make the clock face look like their own faces. They can add eyes and a mouth, and yarn for hair.

4. Help children attach the hands using brass fasteners.

5. As you read aloud each page of the minibook, pause to allow children to arrange their clock hands appropriately.

As an extension, have children write their own "It's Time" books using the text in the mini-book as a model. Invite them to share their books with the class. As they read, classmates can set their clocks to the times in each child's story.

Monster Math School Time by Grace Maccarone (Cartwheel, 1997). Readers will delight in this day in the life of twelve little monsters. The book follows the monsters from the time the monsters wake up for school at 6:00 until they call it a day at 8:00! Clock faces, both traditional and digital, appear on each page.

Animals live in the rain forest.

Where Do Animals Live?

25 Easy Nonfiction Mini-Books Scholastic Teaching Resources

Animals live on the farm.

Where else do animals live?
Animals live with me!

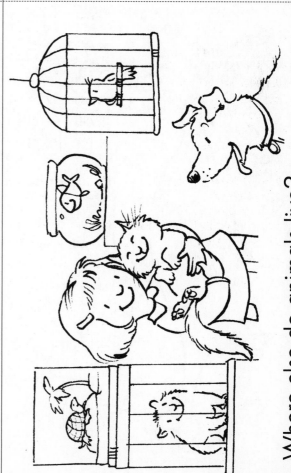

1

Animals live in the woods.

2

Animals live in the pond.

25 Easy Nonfiction Mini-Books Scholastic Teaching Resources

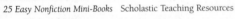

6

Animals live in the sea.

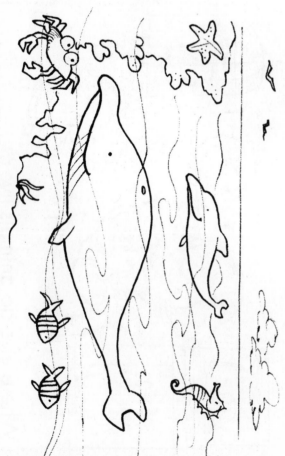

5

Animals live in the desert.

a little sun,

a little water,

A little squint!

How a Seed Grows

a little plant,

What Do You Need to Grow a Seed?

seeds

dirt

water

sun

1

A little pot,
a little dirt,

2

A little more dirt!

a little hole,
a little seed,

25 Easy Nonfiction Mini-Books Scholastic Teaching Resources

6

Parts of a Plant

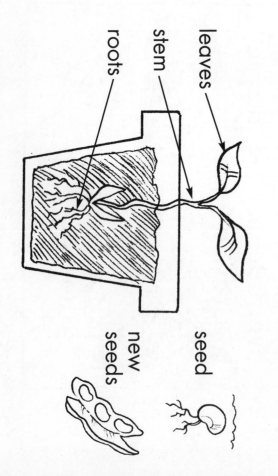

leaves

stem

roots

seed

new
seeds

5

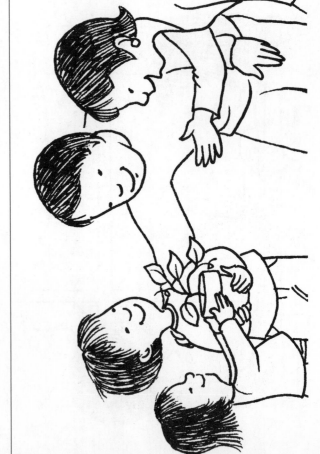

a bigger one!

③ An egg changes.

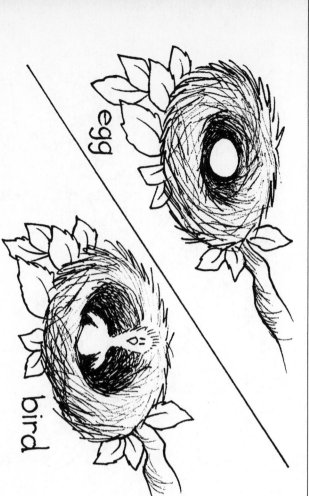

egg

bird

Everything Changes

①

25 Easy Nonfiction Mini-Books   Scholastic Teaching Resources

④ A caterpillar changes.

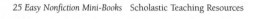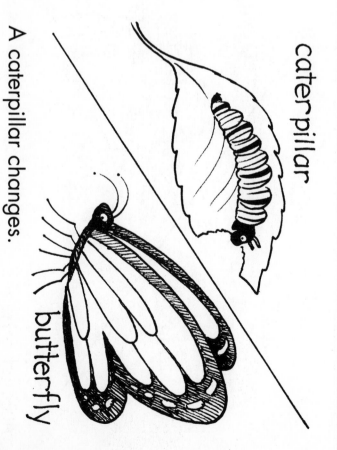

caterpillar

butterfly

Growing Up!

You change, too!

⑦

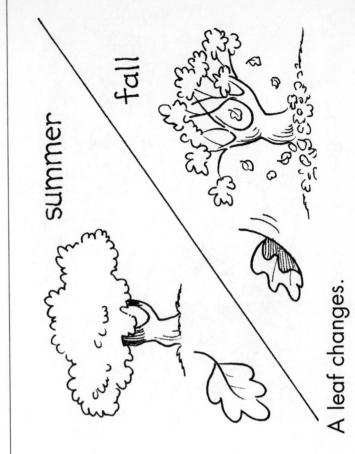

summer

fall

A leaf changes.

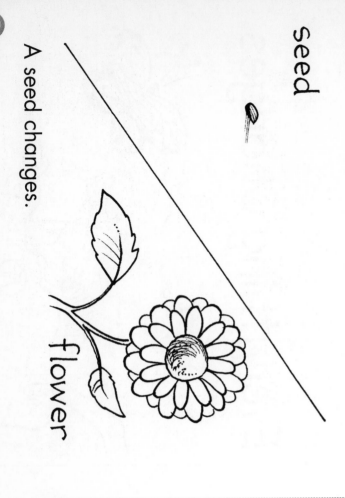

seed

flower

A seed changes.

A cloud changes.

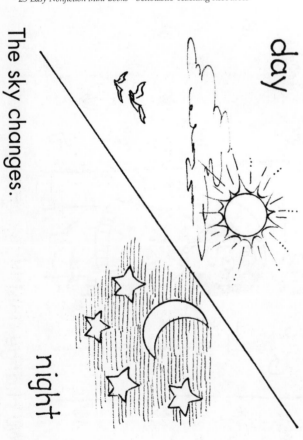

day

night

The sky changes.

A rabbit is hiding in a hole.

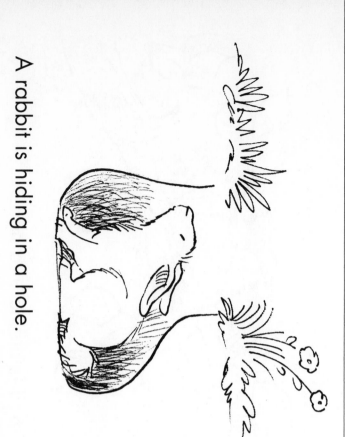

Who Is Hiding?

A snake is hiding in the grass.

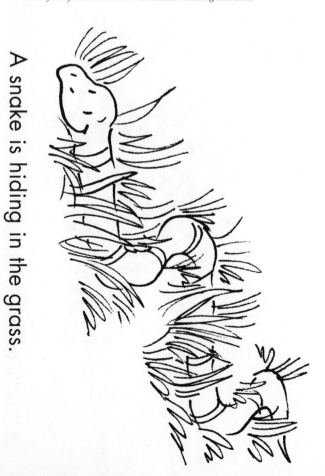

And I am hiding in my tent!

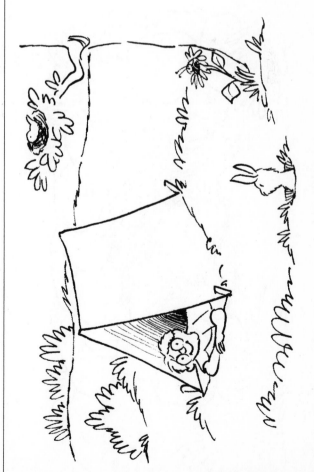

A bug is hiding in a flower.

A bird is hiding in a nest.

A bear is hiding in a cave.

A fox is hiding in a log.

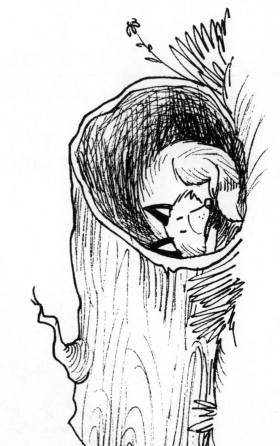

water in the pot,
water to drink.

25 Easy Nonfiction Mini-Books   Scholastic Teaching Resources

Water in the river,

water on me!

1

Water in the bathtub,

2

water in the sink,

6

water in the lake,

5

water in the sea,

Hot days are fun for me.

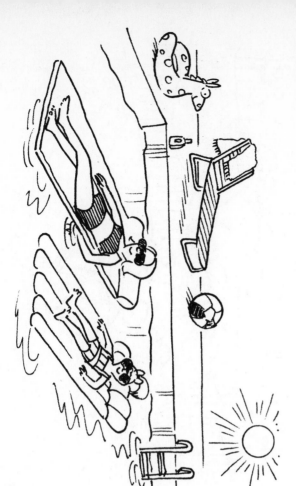

Cold days are fun for me.

All Kinds of Weather

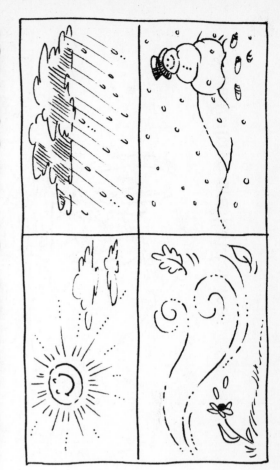

25 Easy Nonfiction Mini-Books   Scholastic Teaching Resources

I like all kinds of weather!

1

Sunny days are fun for me.

2

Rainy days are fun for me.

25 Easy Nonfiction Mini-Books   Scholastic Teaching Resources

6

Snowy days are fun for me.

5

Windy days are fun for me.

I hear with my ears.
The fire truck sounds loud!

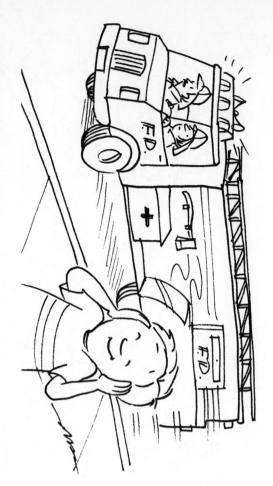

My Five Senses

I touch with my hands.
The rabbit feels soft!

What can you taste, smell,
touch, hear, and see?

I have five senses.

I see with my eyes.
The butterfly looks pretty!

I taste with my tongue.
The ice cream tastes yummy!

I smell with my nose.
The flower smells good!

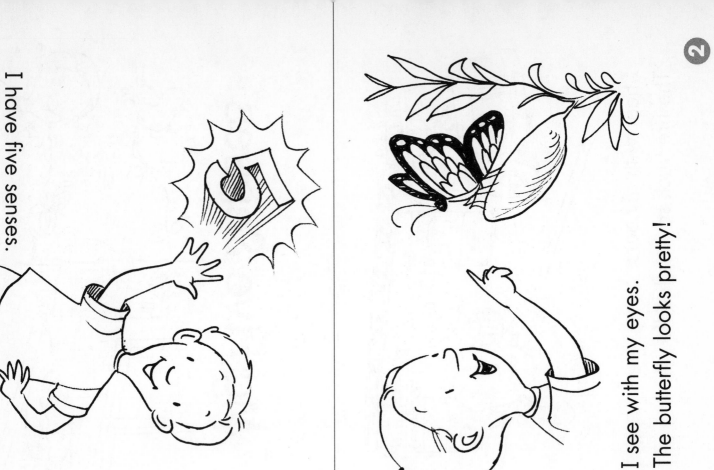

Squirrels need trees.
They eat acorns from trees.

Animals Need Trees

Caterpillars need trees.
They eat leaves from trees.

Animals need trees.
And people need trees, too!

2

Bees need trees.
They make hives in trees.

1

Birds need trees.
They make nests in trees.

5

Beavers need trees.
They use branches from trees.

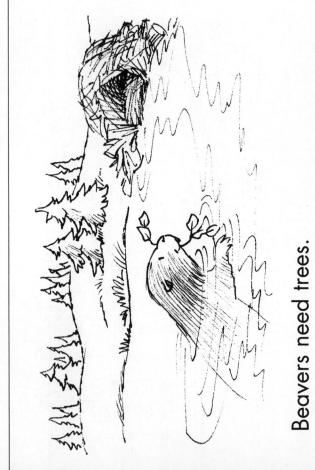

6

Raccoons need trees.
They live in the trunks of trees.

She likes to read.

What We Like

He likes to draw.

We all like to eat!

She likes to skate.

He likes to ride.

He likes to bake.

She likes to build.

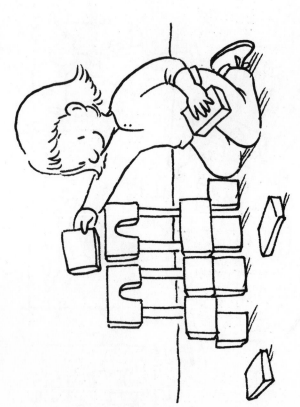

Friends are for reading.

Friends are for talking.

Friends

Friends are for helping.
Friends are for caring.

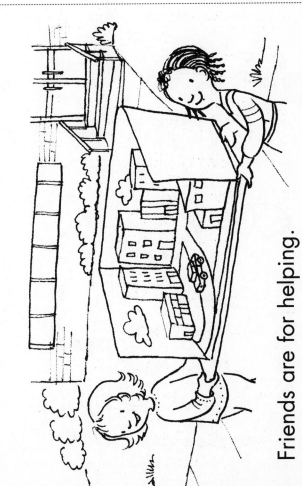

Friends are for meeting.

Friends are for walking.

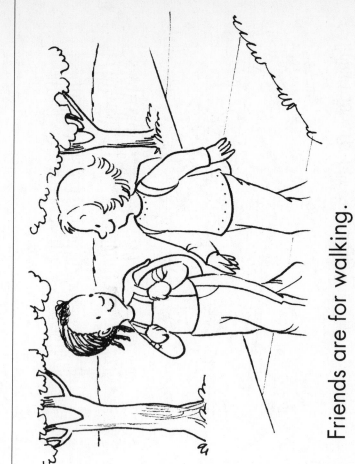

Friends are for sharing.

Friends are for playing.

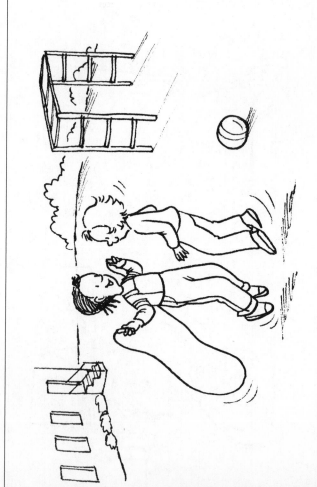

Here is my sister.

My Family

Here is my brother.

Here I am . . . with my family!

Here is my mom.

Here is my dad.

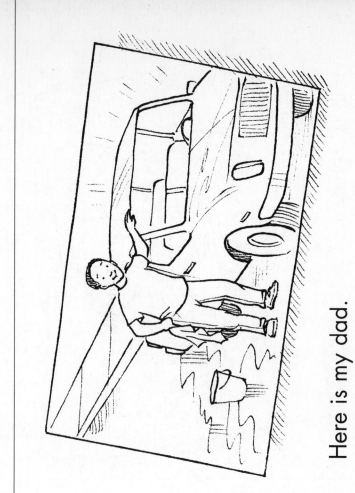

Here is my dog.

Here is my grandma.

3

Families shop together.

What Do Families Do?

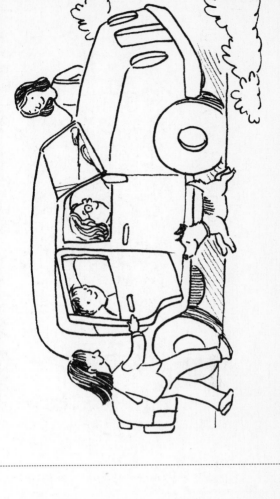

25 Easy Nonfiction Mini-Books   Scholastic Teaching Resources

4

Families eat together.

Families have fun together!

7

1

Families work together.

2

Families play together.

6

Families learn together.

5

Families go places together.

Maybe I'll be a teacher.

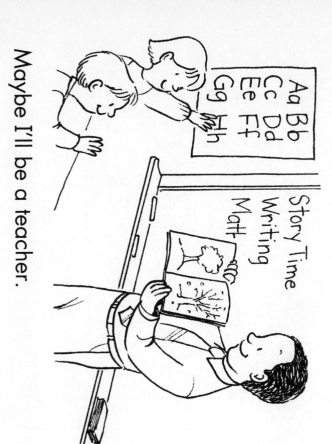

When I Grow Up

Maybe I'll fly a jet.

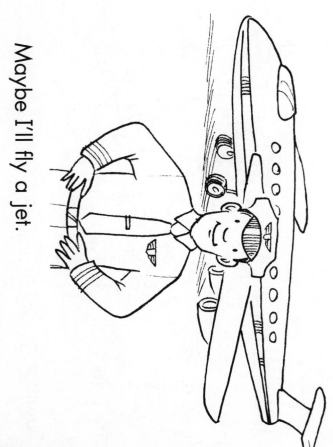

Maybe I'll be a lot of things . . . . but for now I just want to be ME!

Maybe I'll be a firefighter.

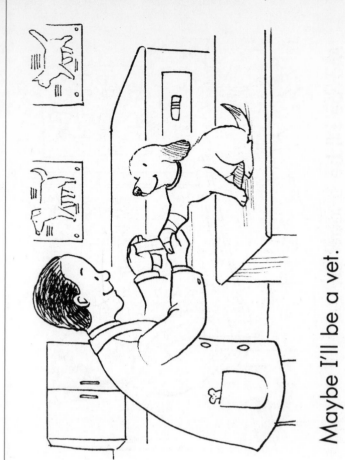

Maybe I'll be a vet.

Maybe I'll be on TV.

NEWS

Maybe I'll be an artist.

A community has parks.

What's in a Community?

A community has people!

A community has a library.

A community has stores.

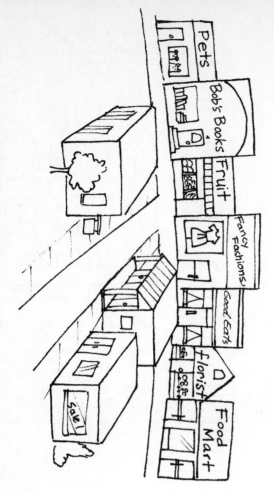

A community has homes.

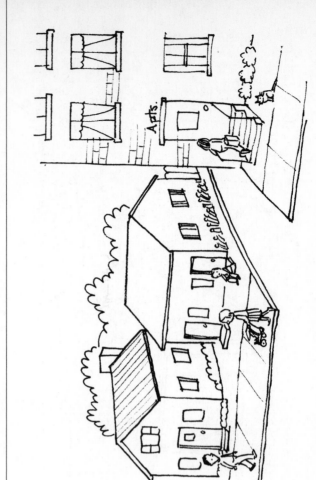

A community has a fire station.

A community has a post office.

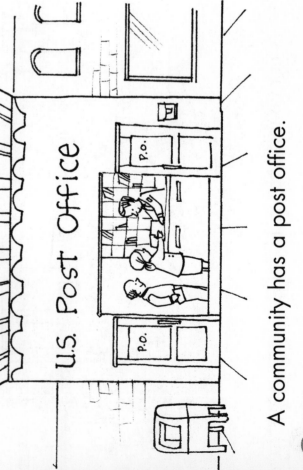

Let's go!
We'll take a boat.

Let's Go!

Let's go!
We'll take a car.

Grocery Store

School

Let's go!
We'll take our feet . . . and walk!

1

Let's go!
We'll take a plane.

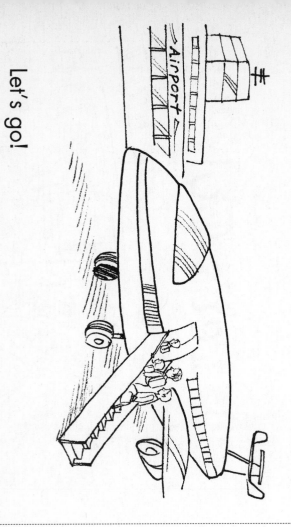

2

Let's go!
We'll take a train.

6

Let's go!
We'll take our bikes.

5

Let's go!
We'll take a bus.

Here is a family today.

Long Ago and Today

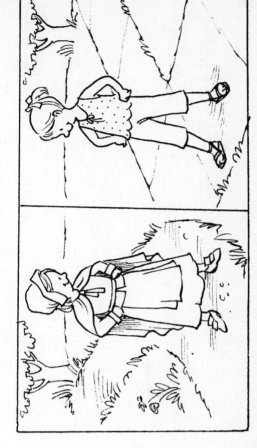

25 Easy Nonfiction Mini-Books   Scholastic Teaching Resources

Here is a house from long ago.

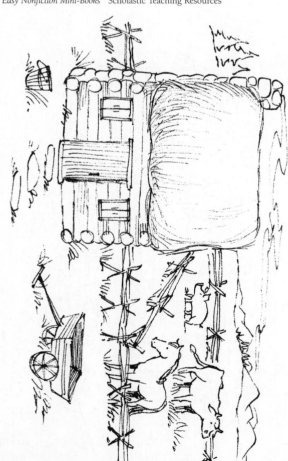

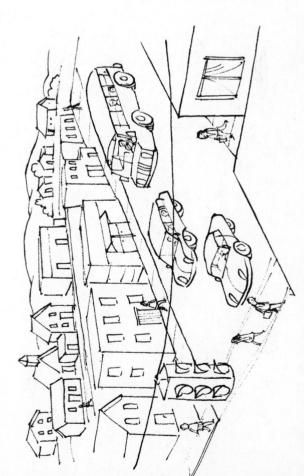

Here is a town today.

1

What was it like long ago?
What is it like today?

2

Here is a family from long ago.

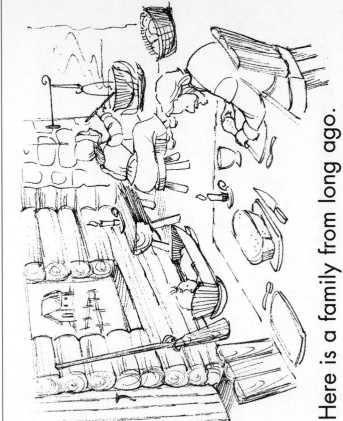

25 Easy Nonfiction Mini-Books   Scholastic Teaching Resources

6

Here is a town from long ago.

5

Here is a house today.

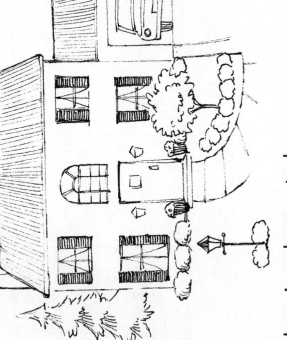

3

America has beautiful deserts.

25 Easy Nonfiction Mini-Books   Scholastic Teaching Resources

America the Beautiful

America has beautiful trees.

4

America has beautiful people, just like you and me!

7

1

America has beautiful mountains.

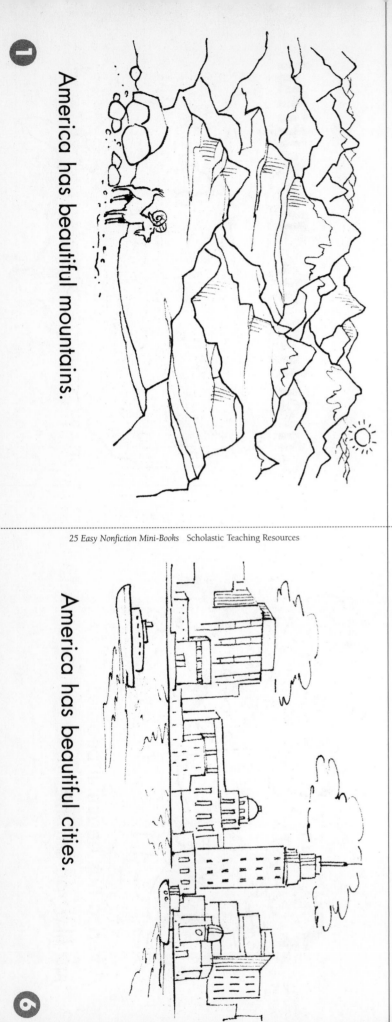

2

America has beautiful seas.

25 Easy Nonfiction Mini-Books   Scholastic Teaching Resources

6

America has beautiful cities.

5

America has beautiful towns.

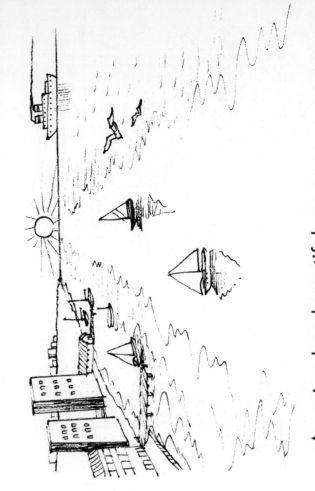

We see squares.

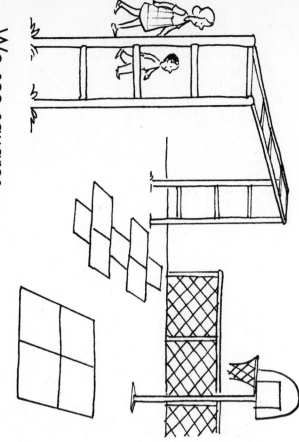

Shape Walk

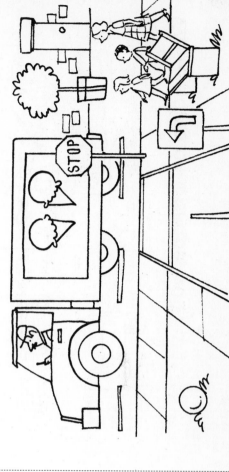

25 Easy Nonfiction Mini-Books   Scholastic Teaching Resources

We see rectangles.

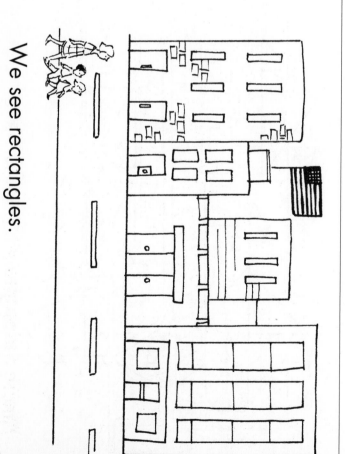

square

triangle

circle

rectangle

Trace and color the shapes.

1

We're going on a shape walk!

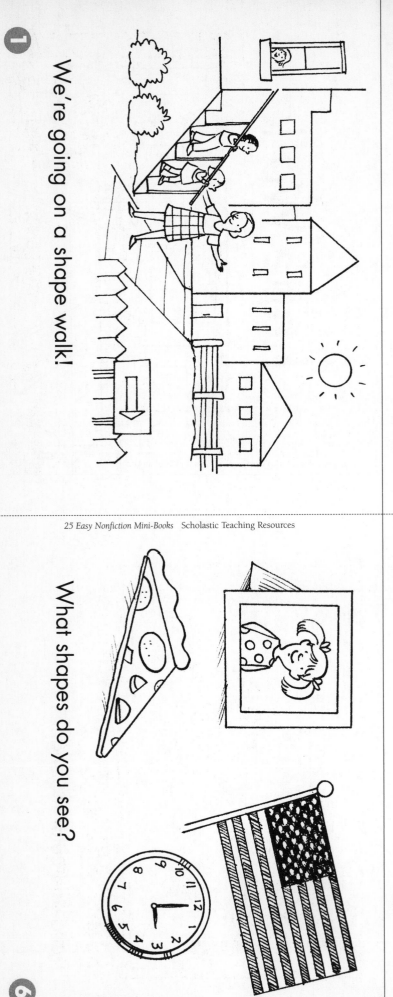

2

We see circles.

6

What shapes do you see?

5

We see triangles.

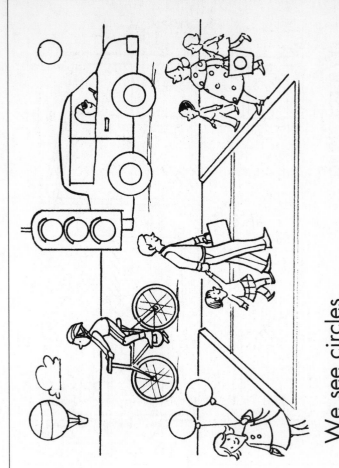
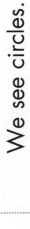
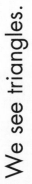

patterns on the quilt,

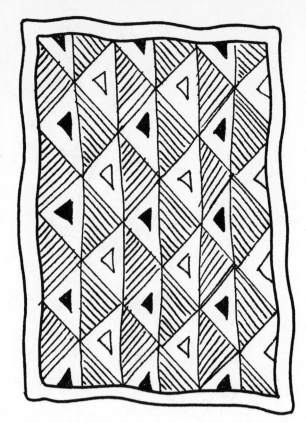

Patterns!

25 Easy Nonfiction Mini-Books   Scholastic Teaching Resources

patterns on the cake.

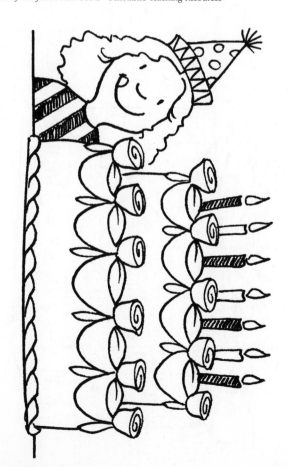

patterns in the sand,
and patterns in the dirt!

1

Patterns on the butterfly,

2

patterns on the snake,

25 Easy Nonfiction Mini-Books   Scholastic Teaching Resources

6

patterns on the shirt,

5

Patterns on the box,

Let's Count!

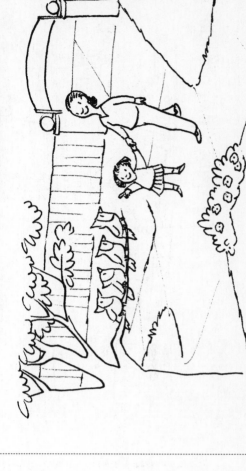

There are six flowers!

1 2 3 4 5 6 7 8 9 10

There are eight dogs!

1 2 3 4 5 6 7 8 9 10

2 4 6 8 9 10

Two, four, six, eight, and ten!

There are four frogs!

10 9 8 7 6 5 4 3 2 1

There are two boats!

1 2 3 4 5 6 7 8 9 10

There are ten steps!

10 9 8 7 6 5 4 3 2 1

PARK

Let's count again! Two, four, six, eight, ten!

1 2 3 4 5 6 7 8 9 10

7 10

Guess how many balls.

25 Easy Nonfiction Mini-Books   Scholastic Teaching Resources

How Many?

---

12 18

Guess how many blocks.

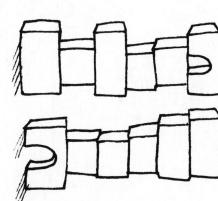

50 100

Look at all the stickers,
and guess how many stars!
Now go back and count!

2

Guess how many rocks.

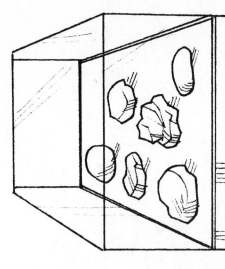

8

6

1

Guess how many shells.

(3) 5

5

Guess how many crayons.

15 **25**

6

Guess how many cars.

16 **36**

3

I spy something soft.

I Spy

4

I spy something hard.

7

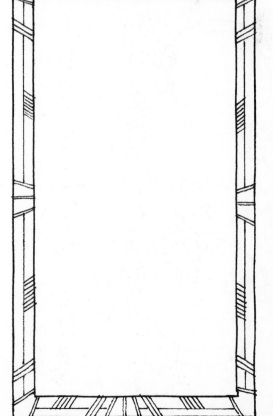

Do you spy something, too?

I spy something _____.

2

I spy something small.

1

I spy something big.

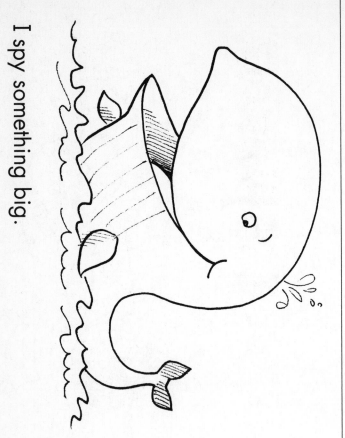

25 Easy Nonfiction Mini-Books   Scholastic Teaching Resources

6

I spy something new.

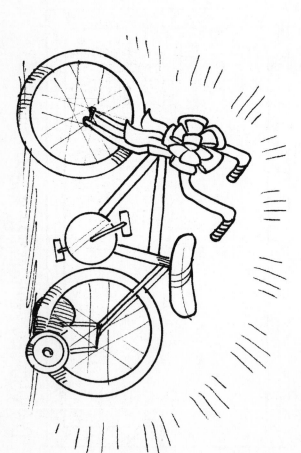

5

I spy something old.

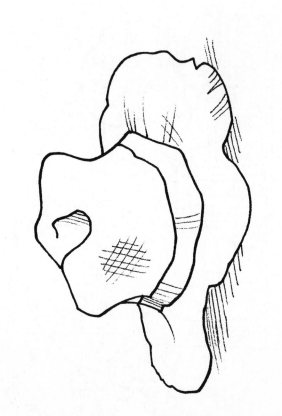

Which is shorter, the boy or the man?

Which Is Bigger?

25 Easy Nonfiction Mini-Books   Scholastic Teaching Resources

Which is taller, the tree or the house?

Which is bigger? Which is smaller? Which is shorter? Which is taller?

1

Which is smaller, the bee or the flower?

2

Which is bigger, the dog or the fish?

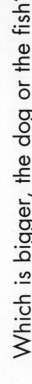

25 Easy Nonfiction Mini-Books   Scholastic Teaching Resources

6

Which is longer, the snake or the lizard?

5

Which is shorter, the crayon or the pencil?

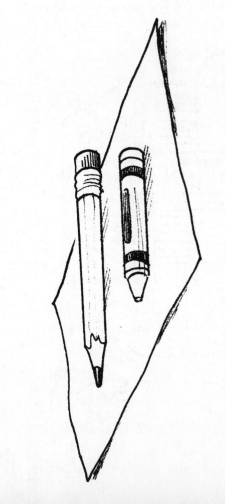

I see 2 big ducks.
I see 3 little ducks.

25 Easy Nonfiction Mini-Books   Scholastic Teaching Resources

Adding Fun

2 + 3 = 5
I see 5 ducks in all!

1 + 2, 2 + 1,
adding can be lots of fun!

1

I see 1 frog on a lily pad.
I see 2 frogs on a rock.

2

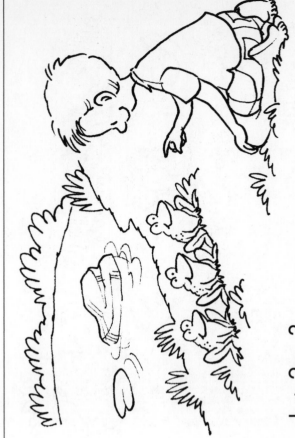

1 + 2 = 3
I see 3 frogs in all!

25 Easy Nonfiction Mini-Books   Scholastic Teaching Resources

6

3 + 3 = 6
I see 6 birds in all!

5

I see 3 birds up high.
I see 3 more birds fly.

It's 10:00.
It's time to read.

It's Time!

It's 12:00.
It's time to eat lunch.

It's 8:00.
It's time to go to sleep.
Good night!

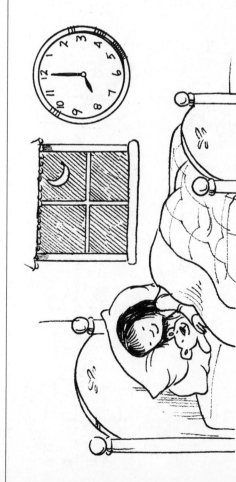

1

It's 7:00.
It's time to get up.

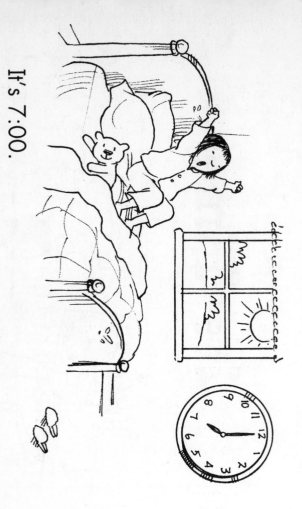

2

It's 8:00.
It's time to go to school.

6

It's 6:00.
It's time to eat dinner.

5

It's 3:00.
It's time to play.